Hert.

Hert.

By

Erik De La Cruz

ISBN: 978-1-7334365-3-3
ISBN: 978-1-7334365-1-9 (ebook)

www.erikdelacruz.com

Concept: Erik De La Cruz
Editor: Omar Apodaca
Front and Back Cover Design: Javier De La Cruz
Back Cover Pop Art Illustration: JMST
Interior Book Design and Layout: Erik De La Cruz

10 9 8 7 6 5 4 3 2 1

Contents

Dedicated

To all the girls that taught me through pain what women are.

To the lost boys who silently suffer in a world that shuns them.

To my parents, who came to the United States from Mexico for a better life, a place where more than just opportunity bred but hardship. For allowing me the liberty to think differently, and the pursuit of changing my circumstances.

My gratitude is self-evident...

To prove this, let Facts be submitted to a candid world. _____

"Who hurt you?"

Her.

My Only Wealth

Addicted to the pain,
Addicted to the love we make,
It feels so good repeating cycles,
Circles like the O's I give you,
We go round and round,
Till we fall in love or lust,
Each other becomes a must,
Attached to the pleasure,
Attached to the suffering,
It feels so good that you're so bad for my health,
I let you steal my only wealth,
My time, you take it all,
You swallow it whole,
As I uncontrollably smile at the ecstasy of it all,
Excruciating fun,
You hypnotized me,
The pain became too unbearable,
We had to be done,
So I walked away,
Only for me to realize my string,
was still attached to you.

Words lead me to you.
I lead you to happiness.
I lead you and you love to follow.
My words lead you to me.
My words lead you to leave.
My words still leave trails of our memories.

The space only left words.
Words are all I had.
Words filled the space.

Words lead me to you.
I lead you to happiness.
I lead you and you love to follow.
My words lead you to me.
My words lead me to new adventures...
My words still leave trails of our memories.

She Said I Need Space

You held a secret,
A secret from me,
As you scoped me out,
You had another,
Orbiting your planet,
I was just one,
Among your belt of debris,
I wanted to show you the universe,
You didn't care,
Attention to your sphere,
Compliments you loved to hear,
You just forgot to mention,
This secret side of you,
You told me who you were,
But your body spoke a different language,
In that, I wasn't fluent,
Your mind with me, flew and went,
Thoughts became asteroids,
You sought to fill voids,
Your orbit was full of moons,
I thought I was your only,
You loved to keep them close enough to almost touch,
Where they'd wish they could hit.

We collided, and it was a beautiful disaster,
If only I'd realize then that it'd spin back to me,
You thought you were a galaxy,
But you were just a waste of space.

Time shows no mercy to her beauty that once was her most powerful asset.

Time is a woman's mortal enemy that burns all hope of everlasting beauty, for even the plastic will eventually melt.

The wrinkles in time are displayed on the faces of women who believed their beauty would be everlasting.

Enchanting was her grace, but ungraceful was her fall from beauty.

Time is the greatest equalizer…

Time shows no mercy to a boy's desire to develop.

Time is the enemy that a boy conquers to then become a man.

The impatience boils within a boy to build himself towards a mission.

Time — for boys it creates a chokehold that suffocates; for men it hardens their inner strength.

Awake Paralysis

Great girlfriend I'd hope you'd be,
You sold me on a dream,
Sleep paralysis it felt with you,
Unable to move,
But awake feeling all the pain,
The scariness, the fear of never waking up,
I was stuck, trapped in my body,
You became the shadow that creeps in front of me,
I was helpless, enduring constant stress,
Under covers I felt suffocated,
Undercover agent for the demons you became,
You sold me on a dream,
What I figured would be paradise,
You convinced me you had the cure,
Became unpredictable, pair of dice,
A game I was set up to lose,
You loved to sell and well you did, unaware I just bought into hell,
You wanted to play by your rules,
I wouldn't allow it,
You were used to playing these fools,
But I was smarter than you,
I knew, you were using me,
I was the safe bet, the insurance policy,
After all the riding of the carousel,
You were ready and set,
To settle,
Too bad,
I left.

Alone, *you wept.*

Her emotions rebelled tradition.

Snake Charmer

The longing of your vicious touch,
Thoughts of you in my mind too much,
The longing of your venomous touch,
You host yourself onto me,
On my skin you etch yourself in,
I try to escape it, or so I think,
But I love it, I don't know why,
You are wicked in your spells,
Your waterfall calls my name,
I dive in unaware of the consequences.

The mental fences you jump over with ease,
An immigrant on my land,
You take whatever I have,
And kill my hopes and dreams,
You latch onto my beauty and deteriorate it,
For your own benefit,
Once you have had your share of enough,
You leave me dead to rot,
To find another,
Why do I even bother,
With women like you,
You took what you could,
In your mind, it's what you should,
do.

In the city of singles,
It's all going to burn,
In the city of singles,
The soma feels so euphoric,
In the city of singles,
The sex brings ecstasy,
In the city of singles,
We use vices in replacement of intimacy,
The grass seems greener,
The moments become perishable,
Fleeting are the feelings,
Fleets of trojan horses break walls put up for preservation,
The walls of women as frail as ever,
The malicious Queen tells all they need not protection,
The women love the thrill of the danger,
Unaware of the horse's hollow shell,
Once deep inside, shallow feels the wetness,
The liberation from purity,
Left the gates open when their last thought is security,
The King poisoned by his trust in her,
For the protectress carried with her two snakes,
For without two eyes filled with venom — still able to see the truth,
The sea brought about his death, for the waves are with women,
The women revolt against his authority,
Destroying their safety,
All for a false sense of liberty,
Unaware of their newfound responsibility,
They choose to feed the flame of no accountability,
The warriors within win for they take all available resources,
The elite forces' cancer spread within the bloodstream of society,

...

...

"I fear women, even those bearing the gifts of their bodies,"
For truth by men is worth death in their serpent eyes.

The horse's womb filled with enraged women,
Burning with hate against themselves,
Broke open, openly broken everyone becomes,
The spark appears temporarily,
Extinguishing generations for temptations,
In the world of singles,
It's all going to burn.

B
    U
R
    N

.

She loves to play house with her dolls,
Dresses them up pretty,
She has conversations with them for hours,
Nothing brings her more joy than playing mom,
She feeds them, puts them to sleep,
Natural were the motions that she saw her mom do,
She became, a mirror, to see herself,
In her imagination there was no one playing daddy,
Reflection of her reality,
Domestic dysfunction,
She stopped liking what she saw in herself,
The playground showed her the girls that got attention,
The girls who acted with what seemed like good intention,
But ruthless were the whispers from behind,
Warfare deeply rooted,
Like telling her she looks cute with short hair,
She longed for acceptance, changed her appearance,
Threw her dolls off her bed, across the room,
Random men threw her mom on the bed, from across the room,
At parties, she makes out with men she just saw across the room,
No bra, no panties,
Locked doors, on the wall a cross in the room,
Yelling God's name in vain,
Followed the storm until she drowned herself,
She cut herself on the jagged rocks,
Her body became cracked,
The tears flushed through her.
"You don't want me. You don't want me."
No one did.
Just like no one did her mother.

Mom tries to kiss her scars,
But it can never be right.

Raccoon

'Men are trash' to you,
Men were raised by women like you,
Women choose 'trash men' to reproduce with,
Then wonder why the trash left on a certain day of a week,
This causes dissonance,
You love the risk, you love to fix,
Realizing you can't fix him,
You should be fixing your nature,
You'll never realize,
You'll never understand,
Emotions are what drive your decisions,
But you love it since you assume no responsibility for your actions,
You're the victim,
The oppressed, the stressed,
The test you've seemed to fail,
Women chose to infiltrate,
To spew hate,
Now men have become women,
And women see no wrong,
Because they're trying to become men,
The universe like that, it doesn't bend,
Ruining our relationships with ourselves,
Our true nature being subdued,
No wonder everyone's depressed.

She's fallen in love with the suffering,
She's fallen so deeply in love with me,
She loves the chase of my attention,
She seeks my validation,
She wants nothing more than to make me happy,
My pleasure brings her pleasure,
She fights for her right to be my treasure,
The suffering brings her the feeling of being alive...

For if I did the same, the opposite would be true,
The reverse isn't true, disgust breeds subconsciously,
She starts to form pity,
For a man to be looked down upon,
Does the opposite of turn her on,
She adores looking up to me,
The second I slip and fall it accelerates her scorn,
The respect depletes, and the bond is slowly torn,
The heart she wore for me proudly falls to the floor,
Like her panties used to before,
Around her ankles she quickly kicked them away,
Now, they act as chains, locked away,
There's no way to open,
Because I became open,
My adore for her poured and it filled her to the brim,
Nauseous of her seeing her own replica,
She's meant to embody the way I've been acting,
Lack of self-awareness — she doesn't see herself,
A man acting as she does breaks her rules,

...

...

She creates rules,
Builds tension to leave to become ruled,
Dissonance within — she's been fooled,
Rancor escalates at her core,
She ran for the lure of being able to suffer once more,
For the bore of neediness is worse than torture,
For the distress of having to guess how you feel,
Makes her mind run wild,
She loves to have to impress, a game of incremental progress,
Your composure will impress,
That is when she will truly begin to obsess.

Broke My Trust

I thought I needed another you,
I thought a lot about all the good of us,
I often forget all the times you broke my trust,

I often don't recall the stress you caused,
It often seems to slip my mind, all the times you made me cry,
I want to forget all the times...

I thought I'd be so lost without you,
I am ashamed I ever thought of you as anything above basic,
It makes me sick that I put you on a pedestal,
It brought great shame for you to look down on me,
When you were never above me,

You were average at best, but you captured my sympathy,

You captured my care, I wanted to heal you,
It makes me mad I wasted so much time on you,
You were another girl that took advantage of me,
I had so much equity in our relationship,
I figured, it'd work despite the b r o k e n,

You were shattered, and I took you in with open arms,
You left the inside of my arms all scarred,
You held long enough for me to have bled my resources,
I tried so hard to keep us united,
It drove me insane, but it was just a game to you,
You never appreciated the genuine love I have for you.

Just another fix for you,
How ironic.

I love(d) you.

You were holding me, not in the ways I wanted to be held,
but in the way that you were holding me back.

I was willing to give her the world, if she complied.

Instead she lied.

Then complained.

Once I left her.

Shooting Uno Mismo.

Unfiltered Shouts / Pesticide

Repeated patterns of pain,
Bickering, fighting, all in vain,
We are going all in,
Sane is what we wish to be,
Dragging each other down,
Inflicting hurt on one another,
Ego fueling the anger,
We're better off without each other,
We can't seem to let go,

We both know, but the drama adds to the show,
Entertained as we're drained,
Our souls have been strained,
So much worse than what we've gained,
How long can this lust be sustained?
Unexplained feelings burrowed in our hearts,
Pride doesn't allow the little things to not matter,
We both want to be right,

Going to bed bitter,
Sleepless nights, texts back and forth,
Unfiltered shouts at each other, repeatedly,
Is this love? Are we doing this right?
We care so much, yet we lose touch whenever we're together,
Are we good as one?
Or are we two separate ones?
Always colliding and it's better that we're done,
The highs are so high,
The lows drown us both,
And it's not for us to purify,
We were good, a lover just to swing by,
We must grow away from the pesticides,
I care enough, to say goodbye.

Thoughts of us from forever ago,
They blend together, a mural of flawless,
How perfect I thought you were,
How pure I thought you were,
How naive my thoughts of you,
Your allure, your smile, your laugh,
Surface was polished,
Under the face, in the skull was empty,
No value in what is available to all,
Nothing valuable to offer but beauty,
You love to follow the crowd,
While thinking you're unique,
Acting proud as if you're not a replica,
You seek drama to make you feel something,
In your head you create this novella,
It stars you, revolves around you,
Everyone is just orbiting you, you plan it,
You're both the victor and the victim,
You're used to getting everything you want,
The privilege of pretty,
The baggage of petty,
Minor inconveniences are catastrophic disasters,

...

...

It was forever ago and you're still the same,
No need to develop change,
No self-reflection, no wrongdoings,
Why change when desperate men take you as is,
All else is to blame, never you,
A victim to consequence,

No consequences you've ever faced,
Pictures of you resurfaced,
I guess, I should preface this with,
I fell hard for you, facedown my ribs broke my heart...
I'm being facetious, you could say,
It was just a facet of deep infatuation,
You could never face yourself,
Even the mirror looked away.

Empty runs through her veins,
She longs for companionship,
She lures for more oxytocin,
She flirts with death in search of more,
Death of her innocence,
She longs for a kiss, she hasn't been the same since,
The pureness of her ability to bond is worn,
The pureness of her heart has been torn,
She's attached herself to the feeling,
She chases after it,
She's become an addict,
She seeks closeness with others that she can't find in herself,
Surrounded by the stresses, it eases,
Temporary comfort, a feeling of bliss,
The calmingness puts her to sleep,
It takes her away from the feeling of having to weep,
She's generous with those that give her what she needs,
Her appetite is insatiable,
She avoids what would bring her the ultimate high,
Instead she births dilemmas that bring her trauma of abandonment,
She avoids creating life by running away from her own,
The cycles breed more need,
She can't handle the labor it takes to fix herself,
She's not done with the fun of mistakes that can't be undone,
She's locked herself in a heartless cage,
She's ruined her capacity to connect,
The chase of oxytocin,
She's been taught only to sin.

She bottles up her emotions,
Chases bottles to empty in clubs,
Never thinking of her nature to feed the bottle to what she can create.

Almost in Love

I almost had her,
But the killer of love is what she ran away from,
Choosing to hide in the darkness of her room and nightclubs,
She'd bled before and she still had scars,
Hidden in tight clothes cutting circulation,
She could never handle the direct pressure,
No wonder her heart was lifeless,
Nothing was ever enough,
No matter how I showed her,
How I showered her with gifts,
We were doomed before I even said "hi,"
She had no problem wasting her genes,
She saw no value in herself,
She told herself she never deserved love,
How could she when the man who was half of her,
Was never fully there with her,
How could she when the woman who was half of her,
Was busy chasing men that broke her more,
Love wasn't a choice,
But she chose to sabotage anything close to it,
She became an assassin with an astronomical hit list,
Learned to kill before she could be,
I was nothing more than a tally,
On her body count.

By Her

She knew I was unbroken,
She sought out to do the opposite,
I wasn't aware, so I allowed it,
She was beautiful, what a disguise,
I was attracted, quickly built ties,
She took advantage, she stole what she needed from me,
Attention, time, attention, affection,
And more attention,
She moaned my name like a sweet serenade,
I couldn't help but fall,
And for that I paid,
A high cost and I lost,
A muse that loved to use,
The energy of the innocent,
Till she found a better source,
And left you way off course,
Shattered in bits unrepairable,
Pain that is so unbearable,
I was hurt by her.

But it made me who I am.

Her body spoke the language of truth;
what she spoke was emotion.

Juego Para Dos (Game For Two)

You sought attention elsewhere,
You went out to drink and smoke,
Every night, same patterns,
Attention from guys became its own high,
You became addicted to the lies,
Trust out the door when you left,
You left it at the bar,
But never was it your fault,
You saw no fault in your actions,
So I would ignore you.

When I took away attention is when you finally cared.
That was your drug.
A fiend for it. You panicked when I withheld it.
You loved the chase, you loved begging for it.
Rebel to invoke a reaction out of me,
When I blew up, you knew,
I still cared for you,
You still had power over me,
But when I continued to ignore,
Is when uncertainty creeped into the depths of your mind,
Running wild your mind, like you'd love to run wild outside,
Insecurity of us staying together ran through your veins,
More rains, cloudy became our relationship,
I would foolishly still forgive,
I kept you around, I thought I loved you, but...

I had my fun too,
I practiced with girls to be better,
For you, maybe... you can say that,
You loved the wild, I couldn't tame you,
But other girls would let me tame them,
They weren't the same as you,
And that was perfect.

I, like you.

You took me for granted,
Granted, you never cared,
You never spared,
My emotions were nothing to you,
You only cared about how I made you feel,
You absorbed all and got addicted,
To my...

You love to stroke my...
Ego and I come everywhere,
you are,
You have me tied to your distance,
This gruesome dance we have,
You don't even give me half,
You expect my whole,
You fill holes within,
I let my huge ego fill them,
Thinking I'm fixing your broken,
But you're setting me up,
Raising me high up,
So I can fall,
And end up broken,
Just like you.

You Left You

The echoes of your love,
Rattle loudly within my mind,
Can't help but think of the memories,
Can't help but think of you,
The good is the only thing that creeps,
I have your heart, I play keeps,
But you go on heartless, filling voids,
You don't think, you react on how you feel,
Impulse you act, off beat is your pulse,
Anyone who gives you attention you let beat.

You lost respect for yourself,
Under a false pretense of "living your best life,"

Your fake friends hype you up,
As you diminish your own value.

Your fake friends hype you up,
As you lower your own standards,
Alcohol gives you a false sense of security,
To deal with no accountability,
You act out, you love to shout,
You lost yourself after me,
You lost... or maybe,
That's just who you were,
I kept you contained — loved... even.
But it wasn't ever enough as you left you destroyed.

The comfort brings her warmth.

She misses the passion of a blazing sun.
She settles for comfort.
She misses the summer.
She settles for the bleak comfortability of security.
She misses the fire that sparked within her body.
She settles so she isn't alone in the frozen winter.
She misses the fireworks inside her.
She settles to raise the ice she's made with lukewarm waters.
She misses the scorching heat that made her want to run naked and wild.
She settles for a piercing cold reality.
She misses the hot mess her life was.
She settles for a cold heart.
She misses the sunny heart of her youth.
She settles with the polar opposite because her heat diminished.
She misses the burning memories that are stored in the attic of
her mind.
She settles for the frigid arctic.
She misses when she didn't feel numb, instead felt stoked with life.

She unhappily settles for the chill after the thrill of chasing the sun.

Dead Flower

My heart is lost,
Unaware of its surroundings,
Lost in a new city,
In a city full of those lost,
Searching for something unattainable,
I was sold on the fable of love,
Jaded by the allure,
Pure intentions,
She had devilish intentions,
Lesson learned,
She shattered my trust,
So, I shattered her heart.

Moved, moved by life,
Stayed complacent she did,
I sought after the impossible,
I believed, I saw it,
I saw it despite the loneliness,
I saw it despite the stress,
I realized the brilliance I was blessed with,
My heart was never lost without you,
My heart was lost when I was with you,
Because I was giving you my heart,
Someone I should've never given it to,
My heart is meant for what I love,
And that's not you.

Sold the dream,
The dream of fantasy,
The dream that's painted so lovely,
I was crazy enough to dream,
Dream of hope, dream of love,
But those dreams destroyed,
They were destroyed the second I put their dreams first,
The second I put the dreams of us first,
The second I put my dreams second...

Time is running out,
Time loved me. Time embraced me.
I betrayed it for thinking I had more,
I took time for granted,
I put (ot)her(s) before me,
I put the fantasy in front of my dream,
I was one with dreams no one could ignore,
I was one with dreams that to the uninspired, I would bore,
I put dreams aside for comfortability,
I put my dreams aside for consistent intimacy,
I ignored the seeds I planted for an Eve,
Losing sight of the job I was destined for,

...

...

I delayed my ascension,
I was swayed from my vision,
Eyesight cleared,
I sought and no longer feared,
The realities brought about epiphanies,
So many, so many of me, so many boys,
They never wake up, they never make noise,
They marry the fantasy and forever show loyalty,
Cater their lives to (ot)her(s),
They lose themselves,
They were taught that,
They never knew any better.
How bitter.

She vulnerably gave me the power to destroy her.

She whispered, "if you must, please do it gently."

Ideally and Opportunistically - PART ONE

Ideally, I loved her,
Opportunistically, she loved me.

I fell for the Disney love,
I was a knight looking to save her,
I longed for my kiss to fix her,
To awaken her slumber,
To awaken her inner lover,
Like one of her animals she bossed me around,
Sewing the stitches of her past lovers,
The slipper wouldn't fit...

A shoemaker I became just for her,
She lacked respect for me,
She'd step all over me,
I'd pretend I was the red carpet,
I let her take my balls,
As she went to the royal ball,
She was never loyal at all,
Once midnight hit,
She left me,
And rode someone else's chariot.

...

...

Fairly, god, another... won,
I did everything, I did all the chores,
I scrubbed the floors,
I washed her clothes,
I cooked the food,
I wonder why she'd rather dance with another,
I assume she's evil,
Withholding love, sex, and attraction,
But I'm acting like a mother,
Like doesn't attract like,
Enslaved, waiting for permission from her,
No wonder,
My heart wishes for a dream,
But that won't make her fall for me.

Especially with no masculinity.

Women fall in love with insanity because it's unexplainable,
like their emotions.

Ideally and Opportunistically - PART TWO

I represented the rose that withers,
Just like how time isn't kind to her,
She knows this,
Her winter is coming,
It's a cold reality she can't face,
She looks away from the reflective glass,
Keeps me contained,
Until she's done with the beast,
Then, forever I become second best,
In her mind he'll always stay,

The beast can't be tamed,
He breaks free from the commitment of a jail cell,
I fill the role,
Willingly close the door on myself,
But my key doesn't fit the hole,
Trapped by choice,
Because of my lack of choice,
She rings the bell, I obey,
Food under the door,
Because I've been a good boy,
She reads my weakness,

I was dumb enough to look at the time,
It told me she was the one,
She let others take her petals,
I was left with thorns,
She built resentment for her past mistakes,
Her beauty that once was is gone,
She has become a beast,
I had so much love,
I let her feast.

Discover the lovely in the sea of madness.

She's lovely when you don't see the madness.

Lovely in the sea of her madness.

Her madness makes her lovely.

Ideally and Opportunistically - PART THREE

Pure,
She had everything,
But a fire inside her burned,
She was tired of being under the misery,
She disobeyed and rebelled against her father,
She never cared what was forbidden or not,
She was willing to run away despite the suddenness,
She told daddy she was in love with him,
She sold her soul for a man,
She sold her soul for some legs,
She had a man tell her, it is better,
where it's wetter,
Since then, she's never left them unopened,
She got tired of her dream world,
Unaware that the human world is a mess,
She listened to older women's advice,
Became a nasty,
And used her body,
language to do the talking,
She told daddy she was in love with him, and him,
So far gone, too late to see the light,
Looking for her true love's kiss in shallow waters,
What an unfortunate soul.

She isn't worthy of a prince,

                                                            Erik.

Hoebbies

It's one thing to cheat,
Cheating would've hurt,
But you did me worse, you cheated in front of me,
And then put the blame on me, trying to turn it around,
You play victim towards me,
But with the other, it was "all in good fun,"
Accountability, you take none, I break it off, I can't get rid of that image,
I don't see myself ever trusting you again, rather than fight for me,
You claim exhaustion,
You claim temptation for affection,
You claim desperation for attention,
There's no excuse for what you did to me, you say you remember nothing,
The alcohol is to blame, you never take responsibility,
You always think everything will be fine,
You always think everything will blow over,
You don't consider it cheating, either way you're unfaithful,
No longer do I trust you, you shattered it,
You long for me, but went for him, claiming it was nothing,
Playing us both, back and forth, I watched all this play out,
Hurt by each of your actions, you disrespected me to the highest level,
You are mine, you knew that, but your subconscious spoke different
thoughts,
Taunted, mocked me with your every move,
Anger I felt, lost I felt...

...

...

You wanted me, but you wanted more than my attention,
You love to flirt, but you don't love yourself,
You need that validation,
Guys to gas you up, you're a gas station,
To fill your empty, you fucked up,
Now you don't know, what to do, what to think,
But you love to be a hoe,
It's what you love to do,
It's where you don't have to think,
Your only hobby,
You're free,
I guess that was the last time you fucked me.

The Loneliness of a Villain

You want me to right my wrongs,
But you wrongly left me all alone,
I thought you were the one,
Slowly I realized there is no "the one,"
You were in the wrong often,
No accountability for your actions,
Lack of impeccability in your words,
But you were always the victim,

You were sinless,
I was heartless,
I called you out on your bullshit,
You would turn nice,
You would turn stubborn,
A flip of a coin,

You spread a negative narrative,
You wouldn't let me live,
Sought ways to dent my life,
You became two-faced,
Be the good guy long enough...
I became the villain,
While you caused this pain,
No one saw you as the wronger,
I was left a loner,
I got used to its silence,
Now, I'm stronger.

Women are destructive,
Women are disloyal,
Women test a man's strength,
Women need lust,
Women need security,
Women need to be loved,
Women need to be treated as disposable,
Women need to be held,
Women need to be choked,
Women like it rough,
Women love pain,
Women hate same,
Women are what they are,
Men can learn them,
Men can beat them at their own game,
Men can despise them,
Men can celebrate them,
They'll still act as such and do them,
Women are chaos,
Men are law and order,
Men need to embrace and put women in their place,
Women love to be handled by the right man,
A boy must become a man.

...

...

A man on his own terms,
A man who creates his own world,
A man who allows a girl to complement,
A man who women can't help but want to help build an empire,
A woman who melts at the thought of his attention,
A woman who willingly does as he pleases,
A woman who learns his desires and does them without being asked,

A woman who will want to care for him and raise his children,
A man who doesn't allow the woman to sway him,
A man who's assertive, dominant, and focused,
A woman who's following his lead, submissive, and respects him,
A woman who feels the luckiest to be with him,
A woman who is grateful of all she is given,
A woman who knows at any moment she can be replaced,
A woman who fights for her place right beside him,
A woman who wears the title of main with pride and as a prize she earned,
A man who doesn't get comfortable and strives for greatness daily,
A man who can protect his woman against danger,
A man capable of rage when provoked but refrains from being evoked.

A man is a man. A woman is a woman.
Nowadays? Let's not get crazy.

Tres Años (Three Years)

I thought you were different,
I thought you were the exception,
I thought you were a girl I would settle down with.

I figured out you were basic,
I figured out you were just the same,
I figured out you were a girl worth nothing more than a lay.

I realized how much time I wasted laying with you,
I realized how much effort I put into trying to fix you,
I realized how stupid I was for giving you an ounce of my energy.

I decided I made a mistake,
I decided I couldn't take the pain of your stagnation any longer,
I decided to leave you even if it hurt.

Looking back, I wasted my potential locking myself up with you,
Looking back, I let a demon siphon my dreams and ambitions,
Looking back, I learned to never let a woman hold my mission hostage.

We began with a blacked-out night,
We ended with a blacked-out night,

You lose them the way you gained them...
                              I suppose.

Underneath it all you just used me,
I was a temporary fix to your issues,
I brought you comfort and you used it up,
A well to you, left empty, it didn't end well,
Fell for your facade,
You fell for me — only temporarily,
Just enough to make you feel something real,
Then poof, it disappeared,
Like you did,
Maybe not physically,
You stayed around,
But mentally you were in the arms of another,
Underneath the body of another,
You were on top of my accusations,
Smooth with your words,
Lies slithered in my ears poisoning me with ignorance,
The high felt like bliss.

...

...

A beautiful untrained actress with an award-winning performance,
She fooled my judgement,
Ran away and stole the show,
Stole my heart,
No guilt or remorse,
As if evil was her source.

Antithesis of What You Sought / The Lost Feminine

Was it even real?
Did you really love me or only fell in love with how I made you feel?
Were you about loyalty?
Why were you so jumpy when I went after your phone?
Did I fit the "safe choice" profile?
Did I check the boxes for a man you'd bring home to your parents?
Were you my biggest fan?
Or were you banking on my potential?
Did you have a game plan?
You became a 20-something with some things you'll take to your grave,
You drowned out your innocence with the alcohol and drugs you've done,
You loved the wild nights and all the fun.

Now your biological clock ticks echo in your mind louder each passing
day,
You noticed me being the antithesis of what you sought all those years,
You tell me that isn't you anymore, just a phase it was,
You regret your actions, never saw the consequences of that at the time...

Now, you can't connect vulnerably with a man,
Now, no man with values and dignity wants you,
Now, you build resentment towards younger women who have what you
don't have, fertility,
Now, you realize that older women told you to be free and have fun for
the sake of living vicariously,

...

...

Now, you realize that the media and the movements lied to you,
Now, you realize a career isn't what you can nurture, no one cares, it is lifeless,
Now, you expect a trophy for living your life like a man,
Now, you expect me to take you as you are, baggage and all,
Now, you understand that it wasn't worth it,
Now, you understand that the legacy of your life dies with you,
Now, you realize that men and women *are* different,
Now, you realize equality *was* a lie,
Now, you regret because you couldn't have it all,
Now, you live unfulfilled, depressed, bitter, while others start families,
Now, you realize the repercussions of that single girl lifestyle fed to you,
Now, you realize you ate too much of it, you've gained so much weight,
Now, the weight of the hate towards yourself and what it is to be feminine is lost on you,
Now, your empowerment powers down, you notice time wasn't kind to you,
Now, your life's clock stops ticking, deathbed, no husband or children to hold your hand,
Then, from what once was an hourglass, there is no more sand.

Now, was the moment I realized that I had to break up with you,
Because even now, is just a phase for you.

I imagined her as the only one,
I portrayed her as the best there is,
I fabricated a love story in my mind,
I perceived it to be true,
I created her into this goddess,
I deceived my mind to wind itself,
I professed an imaginary love,
I construed a false reality,
Another valentine filling her vase,
Her letter, although naturally lying,
I could only really be mad at me,
She laughed at me,
Maybe she didn't directly,
Her rejection was gentle,
But only to later date my enemy,
Taught me the difference between infatuation,
And love,
I gave her the power she never wanted,
She just was, I fought for an illusion,
Countless nights fantasizing,
Not even a second thought in her mind,
I couldn't not think about her each second,
Overthought each interaction,
Thought myself out of every action,
In her world I never existed.
My heartbreak was real,
My first, painful,
Thankful,
The syllables — the words poured!
Unintentional on her part,
But that's when the poet got his start.

You continue to search for even an ounce of me, in every man.
So, on your knees you pray for those ounces to come.

The girl you see from across the store,
Intrigued, you're wondering about her more,
Little do you know,
She is...
The type that loves chasing parties,
The type that loves adding bodies,
The type that loves escaping priorities,
The type that loves running away from liabilities,
The type that loves binge-watching shows and movies,
The type that has no real hobbies,
The type that lies when she says she listens to oldies,
The type that makes herself the victim in all her stories,
A look of innocence deceives.

A period of her life...
Where there were no boundaries,
Where she prayed for her period,
Where she would wake up on strangers' sheets,
Where she sucked on everything passed to her,
Where she blew anything, she could get her hands on,
Where the smoke she blew fogged her reality,
Where alcohol made her do things she'd never do,
Where she'd cut corners and cut lines,
Where credit cards and screens were swiped,
Where she was selfish with everything but her ocean,
Where she acted on emotion,
Where her assets upped her profile,
Where she experimented for attention,
Where she studied her sexuality more than her books,
Where she doesn't fixate on fixing her life but her looks,
Where she reread texts sent a thousand times,

...

...

Where she would sneak in and out of windows,
Where she would come home as the sun rose,
Where she knew the exact angles in which to pose,
Where she covers her sorrows with purchasing clothes,
Where hellos lead to foreshadows,
Where you go up and introduce yourself...

You hit it off,
Like when she used to take hits,
And take layers off,
And she tells you that part of her life came to a close,
Or chooses to never tell you at all,
Until you fall and she opens parts of her,
She never imagined herself falling this hard,
She says she's done with that life,
She says she's no longer that girl,
She says that girl made mistakes, or choices,
But you're left with no choice but to accept,
She says that you're a guy she never expected to earn,
She tells you that you're worth giving up that lifestyle for,
She no longer desires it,
Because she's found you.

...

...

She knows her beauty is fading,
She's adding weight,
She wants to check out of the dating race,
Her womb is telling her to pick up the pace...

She'd hate to lose you,
Not because you're what she pretends to love,
But only for what she sees you useful for,
As a tool to breed,
And a provider of the water needed to grow the seed.
But more importantly,
For this lifestyle that fits her new needs.

Love My Insides

It's what's within that matters, she says.
Like the flowers she wore as a crown...
She wanted her sexual nature to flourish,
It's what's on the inside that matters,
She tells these so-called men,
Knowing well she only cared about what goes inside her,
She was unleashed to discover herself under the covers,
Emotionally unstable, no regards to being faithful,
Emotionally unavailable, runs from love she doesn't deserve,
She wanted love, drugs, sex,
With no judgement and responsibility,
She could never choose one,
Indecisive so she chose all of the above,
Her body was her choice,
Men chose her body,
But never chose her,
But her body suffered from the choices she made,
When her beauty fades she has to compensate with qualities,
Something that to her was never even a foreseeable part of her worries,
So-called men deceived to accept her with open arms,
Where once she was free to love with open legs,
Free love, to love freely became a con,
Doomed are the lowest of men,
Love me for who I am, she tells these men.
She wanted her rights to... but devastated when she was left,
Alone,
She could love him more than anything,
But never more than her freedom,
So what's what she chose,
No man could love her insides,
There was nothing inside.

The Punishment of Mother's Choice

Her life was fatherless,
So, she grew up heartless,
Once she grew up, in strangers' rooms she became dressless,
Resentment fueled her drive,
The journey to arrive at happiness,
To no avail, but it didn't stop her from trying to prevail.

She never knew authority,
When a man would try to control and set rules,
She fled,
Ran away towards the arms of boys who would let her do as she pleases,
She cried on their shoulders and they accepted,
She loved men who were willing to leave at any moment,
That anxiety drove her crazy in love,
It reminded her of her childhood,
Watching her dad's truck drive away for years or forever, she never knew,
In and out of her life,
Like the men that came in and out of her legs.

...

...

She was stubborn, no one could tell her right or wrong,
She was certain she was right always,
Despite all the ways she would consistently screw her life up,
She lived the punishment of her mother's choice,
But problems of that she never would voice,
Her mom was just as much a victim as her,
Her mom vilified her dad, all she ever knew was the bad,
What if her dad tried to find her?
What if her dad found out mother was cheating,
What if her dad tried to be a part of her life but mother wouldn't let him,
What if the family courts ordered he not try or even get close to her
because of mother's lies,
What if he tried everything to no avail.

Once she grew up and became available, the damage had been done,
Hate in her heart for her dad pumped through her veins,
Her lack of trust in men remains,
What if she's always tied to the chains of her mom's poor choices,
What if she's consistently falling victim to her learned vices.

"Stop being such a bitch. Act like a man!"
She'd yell at me as I cried to repair what was broken.
Overly emotional, to lose her I was fearful,
I couldn't take the insanity,
All she brought to my life was instability,
She would hit me with harsh words,
I'd do anything to bring her self-esteem up,
I thought I became the problem,
Slowly, I changed myself to avoid the impulsivity of fights,
But it only worsened,
I didn't understand, I was becoming the man she wanted,
I could never amount to the man her father was,
I was the opposite of him.
I was scared to leave her unlike him,
She knew I was weak enough to control,
Insecurities bled into my relationships with her worries,
Cutting attachments to girls I'd been friends with,
She was worth more than those girls, so I saw no issue,
But along came the use of more tissues,
Her problems became my problems,
There was no satisfaction, there was always more to rip from my core,
But I loved her, I thought to myself,
We had invested so much time, let's add more.

The sabotaging began where family now turned enemy,
Tainted relationships for a relationship destined to sink,
I was scared to jump, I self-sabotaged,
She jumped to another man,
I was weak, weary, and worn out,
Absolutely destroyed, a lost boy unloved,
What was there to live for?
I thought it was over.
I wanted it to be, it was easier than having to start over.

You had a beautiful pearl in your oyster.

You gave it to one.

He took it.

You let it happen.

You imagined you still had it.

Trying to give it to the others that came by.

But they all left quick.

You wondered why.

Lonely you became.

They found no value to stay.

There was nothing worthy of opening it.

For once it's opened, the damage cannot be undone.

Your prize you gave away recklessly.

You spent the rest of your world trying to recoup your pearl.

But to no avail. *You spoiled.*

I knew her body,
Better than she knew her own body,
She was used to anybody,
Who treated her like any body,
Freedom is what she wanted to embody,
Reality is, to claim her was wanted by nobody,
Claimed she was guarding her body,
But the walls of her body building crumbled,
She sought attention from everybody,
She gave herself to everybody,
Tied her lips on any man close enough to her hips,

I made her body feel sensational,
I made her body feel things she's never felt before,
I made her (be)come a body of water,
An ocean, a puddle, she lay in it,
I loved to see her sea make tidal waves,
I loved to make splashes,
She loved to see O's too,
We became so close-knit,
I loved to swim, to row,
I would take what she most needed, oxygen,

She wanted to flood every part of me,
The waves were swell,
The breaking came from the shallow,
Something she didn't forecast...

...

...

I got my cycle,
Surge of emotions,
She poured oceans,
She expected more,
Love is what she waited for,
Why swim in one when I know there's four,
She was a hor-
-rible hurricane,
But she was a sight to explore,
I collected a body of evidence,
Her body text told the story,

The irony is...
She became part of my body of work.

Collection of Sources

I can't get her off my mind,
Her head was brilliant,
She blew me away with her facts,
Her mouth a library,
My pen would ink every page,
Whiter became her pages,
Brighter I would make her days,
I became a highlighter as I came over her words,
She loved to talk,
Whenever I wanted to learn more,
She would open up, I had a pass,
She wished I was a bookmark, so she could have me inside all the time,
She knew how much I loved deep reading,
She loved that I was so willing to read her every chapter.

Little did she know, I was an avid reader,
She should've been smart enough to know,
It slowly seemed to bother her,
She chose the bliss route,
I was curious to know what everything was about.

There were other libraries...
I was checking out.

She doesn't want to hear the truth,
They don't want to hear the truth,
Their truth is less painful than the real truth,
The lies they tell themselves ease their liability,
Go against the lies in their mind, you're an enemy,
Regurgitate their lies back to them, you're an ally,
She wants validation for her reality,
A matter of perception created from deception,
She doesn't want to be tried for her actions,
She defends her lies as if she was battling life,
As if she was under oath to their manifesto,
Recite the lies enough times...

Truth — a wandering that is divine,
Is it a lie that the feminine is divine?
To redefine and intertwine the facts,
Soundbites they spew, lies disguised as what's true,
Far from the truth, we're fed bullshit,
Their words a smokescreen to what they desire,
Ideologies attempting to overtake our biologies,
They construct truth to fit their needs,
Spew toxins onto the growing seeds,
They speak with a forked tongue,
Eating away at truth, they rewrite history,
She sows disinformation and exaggeration,
She avoids consequences, holes in her memory,
Writes herself as the victim in the story,
Her behavior is unpredictable due to the lies,
She flows with temptation leading to her broken,
Their real truth is behind what is not spoken.

Words Cut

Was I scared to love her?
Why was I so afraid of commitment with her?
In her eyes I was a coward,
In my eyes, all I saw was going forward,
She loved to stay in place,
That's not where I wanted to go,
I wanted to elevate to higher levels,
All she wanted to do was get high,
What if I never did love her?
What if I just cared so much about her that I couldn't let go?
What if I was to her a prize to show?

I wasn't a coward, but I was afraid of being judged,
Did I become attached because she was my best friend?
Was I more afraid to lose her completely? So that's why I stayed?
Did I latch on to her because she was nostalgia of who I used to be in high
school?
Was I afraid to grow up and leave it all behind to become great?
All she wanted to do was get drunk,
I got intoxicated from my ideas making money,
What if I was treating her like a failing startup I needed to save and take to
IPO,
I'm pissed off that I wasted so much time of mine,
I cared too much, she loved my care,
Vampire'd the energy for her own ego,
I will forever be her greatest lover,
I don't think I ever fell in love, I fell in guilt.
Guilt of outgrowing her and those I love.

...

...

I was always the nice guy that people loved to take advantage of.
Maybe she thought that... that was what she was getting with commitment,
But I slowly formed into the man she hated to be in love with,
So deeply in love she became, addicted to my love making,
Addicted to my kiss which brought her bliss,
My words cut like how I cut her out of my life,
Shame, shame, so much fucking shame.
That's all my life consisted of.
Then, you wonder why I was a coward to love.

I made you cry a lot.
I made you laugh a lot.
I made you feel.
That both scared you and brought you excitement,
You weren't used to feeling so deeply.

...

...

Your tears fell, I hope they kissed your cheeks for me on the way down.

She Grew

We started with the proper chemistry,
It escalated every single moment we shared,
We fell into this wonderful whirlwind of passion,
We couldn't keep our hands off each other,
We couldn't keep our lips from touching one another,
You couldn't wait to have me inside you,
You couldn't wait for the ride that was about to take place,
I couldn't wait to hear my name said aloud by you,
I couldn't wait till your body was shaking in your own puddle,
You couldn't wait till I finished, I stared at your beautiful face,
You love when I would come, over, you.
When we locked eyes, we shared memories telepathically,
You wouldn't be able to stop yourself from laughing whenever you were with me,
You loved the surprise dates I would take you on,
You loved the attention to detail and gifts I would give you,
You grew to love me.

You said you were grateful to have me in your life,
I believed you. I believed your words.
Until your actions started telling me different stories.

...

...

We fell into this horrifying whirlwind of toxic,
We refrained from touching one another,
We chose to use our mouths for yelling instead,
You couldn't wait to leave my side and be alone inside your room,
You couldn't wait to get out of the car ride,
I cringed at the sound of my name said aloud by you,
I still left your body shaking in your own puddle, but the occurrences lessened,
You couldn't wait till our hang out was finished, I stared at you walking up your driveway,
You hated me coming over because it would lead to fights,
When we locked eyes, they were filled with fury and pride,
You wouldn't be able to stop yourself from crying whenever you were with me,
You hated that I became infrequent with the dates I would take you on,
You hated the overbearing attention I would bombard you with when you were out,
It, lack of trust, escalated every single moment we shared, I couldn't trust you.
We ended with waned chemistry,
You grew to hate me.

Truth is she loves me,
Truth is she hates that she does,
Truth is she'd rather lie than go deep,
Is there any truth to her words?
She loves my smell, reminds her of happiness,
She loves that she can't predict me,
She loves that I am nowhere to be found,
She loves that I'm volatile,
She loves that women eye me from across the room,
She loves that she must bring her A-game,
She loves to know she can lose me at any moment,
She loves that I do as I please,
She loves that I please her so well,
She loves to please me, pleasure it brings her,
She loves that I don't reply or answer her calls,
She loves my mystery,

...

...

She loves my drive and focus,
She loves to think she can change me,
She loves the challenge I bring her,
She loves that I don't care what she thinks,
She loves that I choose the place we eat at,
She loves that I don't tolerate her tantrums,
She loves that I ignore her when she misbehaves,
She loves to be on her best behavior,

She loves to love me,
She hates that she loves me,
She lets hate mean love and love mean hate,
She loves that she never means it when she says she hates me,
She loves that I make her feel,
She hates that she's inexplicably attracted to me,
She hates to tell the truth,
But her body does anyway.

She is capable of both strength and sadness,
She is capable of both love and evil,
She is capable of being both an angel and a devil,
She is capable of saying she loves you while she hides in shadows,
The shadows moaning another man's name,
She comes, home, acting as if all is the same,
She is capable of the darkest when you only see light,
She is capable of being heartless beyond belief,
She's capable of removing guilt from her mind,
She's capable of hiding it for you to never find out,
She's capable of swallowing more than her pride,
She's capable of staying with you for comfort,
While she keeps a lover on the side,
A side she loves to ride for the thrill,
She throws you a bone when you're starving,
She gives him a treat anytime he wants to eat,
She can't lockdown this man, so she stays with you,
You and him fill the two sides of her,
You think you have her down to lock a future together,
She wants the best of both worlds with no repercussion,
She doesn't care about causing destruction,
She can't control her temptations,
Doesn't matter what you see or saw,
She keeps you both at a balance like a seesaw,
You don't bring her the same lust,
She's never in the mood, all you get is attitude,
She claims you're not doing enough to make her happy,
She portrays herself as a victim, you panic and do as she pleases,
But you, she never pleases,
She repeats that trust is the most important thing in a relationship.

...

...

She has a strength of lying,
Lying with him, lying to you,
All she does is create sadness,
Self-sabotage, a true love mirage,
Oh, how lovely love could be.

Inside Man

It's crazy how she was here,
But now she's left.

The day she left, she said, I would thank her one day.
I was left in pulverized dust from the surprise attack,
All those years just gone, there was no longer any us,
But I'll remember that day forever,
She told me pretty lies of following her dreams,
How she was doing me a favor by leaving me,
I, like an idiot, believed her, I saw the beauty in her intention,
As I cried from losing her from my life.

I did everything a boyfriend was supposed to do,
I checked every box that I'd been told women want in a boyfriend,
I had no choice but to let her go,
I did everything I could to win her back,
Each passing day, each text, each letter I wrote,
More and more she would pity me, lose respect for me.
My only strategy was to guilt trip her into taking me back,
How pathetic I was.

I realized that bled into the relationship before she left,
Slowly her heart pulled away from me,
Her heart became vulnerable for theft,
I assumed my security was unhackable,
How stupid I was.

...

...

In the tail end of our love, she began to shift her love to another,
I had forever in my eyes that I was blinded by the obvious,
She was devious, finding excuses to see him,
It destroyed me.
I slowly realized I was no longer a man to her, but a sensitive child,
She never left to follow her childhood dreams,
She left to chase the man of her dreams,
A man who in her eyes was better because he was everything I was not,
She never realized she stripped everything from me,
My confidence, who I was, my identity,
Because all that became attached to her,
When she left, I became a stranger to myself,
I guess, it's the past,
Just a story I tell myself.

BIG SISTER KEEPS TABS ON ALL THOUGHT.

She became a master at breaking poet's hearts,
Doing her part in inspiring the arts.

2084

Free or happy?
We allowed it on ourselves,
Free or happy?
Which do we prefer for ourselves,
What is freedom when they define it?
Free but doomed by our own desires,
Happy but only temporarily,
We allowed it on ourselves,
What is freedom when the telescreen portrays it?

Sentimental and imprisoned by our own mental,
The grief of joy is too much to bear,
The shame of excitement too much to handle,
The remorse of elations ecstasy,
The warm sorrow of peace of mind,
The melancholy of prosperity,
The gloom of paradise's solace,

Free or happy?
The serenade of the upgrade is obeyed,
The delayed evade of what makes us afraid,
We betrayed the clichéd love for the accolade,
To be worth more than just what is meant to biodegrade,
Last more than the shade that fades when the sun sets,

...

...

Mass-produce the recluse within the tube,
Induce temptation, diffuse revolution,
Refuse thought, introduce separation,
Induce doctrine, produce ruin,
Loose union, loose feminine,
Ruse consumption, educe depression,
Feminine extinction,
Masculine castration,
Sexual unrestriction,
A misfortune the inhuman and broken...
Him and Her.

Enslaved and somber.

Scarlet Blood

Her inferno burned with ludicrous lust,
Her husband away fighting for honor and justice,
She was bound to nothing as if released,
Sought to paint the town red,
Her lipstick on the chests of men ready to die for her,
The chilling of her soul,
Never stopped her from taking off her clothes,
She cared not of her worth,
In the eyes of the town,
Her fire spread, his seed spread,
Inside her oyster birthed a pearl...

At one point, she'd be burned at the stake,
Now, she's coddled for her mistake,
Her husband double-crossed,
She wears her letter proudly,
Tells the world the valid excuse of "I was lonely,"
Her husband stuck at a crossroads,
Raise another man's child and fall in line,
As if he wasn't on the front lines manning up,
She has countless men waiting in line,
Out of wedlock, no real consequences,
The gavel in her court,
Despite a child, desperate men they court,
She believes she is strong and capable,
Unaware of the detriment that can cement in a child's mind,

...

...

Lack of father figure because of her lack of composure,
Lack of father figure because of her lack of resistance to pleasure,
Lack of father figure because she's a cheater,
Weak men fill holes of the vacancy left post-divorce,
She exposes her child to her reckless behavior,
False claims of father not around because she's hard to tame,
She raises a child to be wild like her,
A supportive friend, no discipline on her end.

She no longer takes the steps to the guillotine,
Instead she guillotines temporary stepfathers.

Obsessed in fighting for freedom she already has,
No remorse when there is no power to enforce,
No presence of discipline,
She painted the world scarlet with sins.

Women followed in what they figured were wins.

Take off your wings,
Place them on pillows of strangers,
Where your knees would go,
You, under his eye,
Blessed be the fruit that he bears onto you,
She wipes away her conscious,
She hides these tales,
Tells no tales of exposing her own tail,
Her innocence left in ruins,
Mentality of ruin is a gift,
Ruin is the road of transformation,

She is bound to nothing,
Longing for the sweetness of doing nothing,
Doing nothing but doing others,
All in good fun, she never believed in love,
Seeking rejuvenation in temporary temptation,
In fleeting lustful emotion,
Her power in bonding with a man, broken,
Annihilation of self-valuation,
Attempting to receive validation,
She never wanted these men,
She let them in anyways,
She wanted them,
Attraction is unexplainable,
Her body lusts even after what she doesn't trust,

...

...

A man who pays her no attention,
She's charging you, hoping you swipe to purchase,
He's allowed a free trial,
Follows up with the transaction,
Her return policy is lenient,
An exchange of some lust and a bust,
An exchange after realizing the damaged goods,
He didn't realize what was in store,

Suffered from the sisterhood's falsehoods,
She lay broken,
On her back, on her chest, her crossed hands,
In the bed she made.

BIG SISTER TOLD HER SHE WAS A PURESLUT.

A woman with too much freedom is a liability to society.

Wanderlust

She loves to travel,
She loves to get away from the stresses,
She loves to chase the new,
She loves the experience of the new,
She says she's in love with you,
Yet she loves these escapades,
She says she loves to explore,
She seems different even distant,

You ask... "who're you?"
Never realizing you should take out the apostrophe,
Take away the 'you' from her life,
There is no question,
Add an exclamation,
Her love seems to be going through a contraction,

Everything she says and does, contradiction,
She leaves with a small suitcase,
She comes back with all this extra baggage,
You wonder why you must deal with it,
You've run out of room for her baggage,
Yet every time she comes, back she's emptier,
She says she loves to breathe the new air,
She says she loves to dock herself in new ports,
She loves being away from her job,
Away she blows...
Meeting guys in places where her, no one knows,
You believe her words, she's faithful,
Only time she's full of faith,
When the plane meets some turbulence.

//

She says it's just a girl's trip,
You can't be that guy and be insecure,
No cure for her indecency,
She loves to be free,
They can't judge her,
They can't tell another,
They probably don't even know her real name,
But what you'll feel is real pain,
Once you connect the dots on the map,
The state of your relationship is faltering,
She loves to experience the journey,
You are pressured to see no fault in her actions,
She never has to make amends,
She finds herself in foreign men,
She loves to be on her knees saying amen,
To the new blessings she's been given,
An opportunity to explore new and still be with you,
She loves to travel,
The truth, you'll never unravel.

She believes…
She believes there is more out there in the world,
She believes her life has a greater purpose.

She gets bored — worse than death in her eyes,
She lies, she cheats,
Her friends don't judge her, for they do the same,
Say they love him but love the thrill of the secret,
They support her, they help her sabotage,
If they're single and alone,
They don't want to be alone in the pain,
Entice you, led you astray,
A stray on the streets she becomes,
They lure you to join them in the dumpsters,
It's tempting to join when they paint it well,
They go looking for colors,
They go looking for brushes,
Alone in their world of black,
Their eyes become painted just the same,
A thousand lost dreams in her eyes of love,
She never knew anything about love,
She only knew her beauty could bring her abundance,
She never cared for the romance,
She just wanted the value, the rest made her sick,
She just wanted the—
Disgust brought her the romantic.

...

...

All of this used to bring her shame,
All of this she isn't proud of,
All of this lack of self-love,
All of this rationalized as part of her journey,
All of this is part of her self-discovery,
All of this, a canvas to paint her as she really is,
Full of so many splattered paints,
For within her, there was never light,
Black — her soul.

The bestest of friends they said they were,
Enemies these women became,
They smiled at each other,
They complimented each other,
"You look really pretty," is what they tell each other,
But behind the back display their true attack,
Smiling assassins.

Confident, ambitious, glamorous,
Cold, shiny, hard plastic,
Use their pink to gain power daily,
Creating rules that aren't real,
Cynical intensity in their eyes,
With a fire that could burn book(s),
Masters at weaponizing relationships,
Spreading rumors and lies,
About anyone attempting to overthrow or even tries,
The hottest boys on their arms become toys,
Badges of validity in a lawless world,
Ex-boyfriends on-limits in a lawless world,
All is for share in love...
And war brings out what is rotten to the core,
Girl world was never at peace — only pieces,

...

...

Perfect girls with insight on the enemy,
Mean girls full of secrets,
Ill-tempered girls raised by cool moms,
Malicious girls empty in their hearts,
In a world they created,
Untouchable, but understand the fragile walls they've built,
Become perfect is their mantra,
Bored out of their minds,
Out of their mouths words spewing drama,
Girls want no part, but worse is not being part of it,
To be personally victimized is to be a person,
For any attention is belonging and that matters most.

Queen bee with salty honey,
At the mercy of the colony,
She stands at the top of the stairs staring at the chaos she created,
Women with psychological blades that cut sharper than any man could,
Get in, sister...
They're going self-gender sabotaging.

A lost boy looking for love,
A lost boy seeking respect,
A lost boy seeking sex,
A lost boy seeking purpose,
A lost boy looking for guidance.

A lost boy not knowing self,
A lost boy shamed for what he is,
A lost boy taught and raised by his mother,
A lost boy who morphs himself to the reflection of mom's dominance,
A lost boy who feels the spite of his mom's need to wear the pants,
A lost boy who grows to resent his dad for not being around,
A lost boy told he should be more like a girl,
A lost boy told he should be more obedient,
A lost boy drugged to suppress his urge for adventure and conquest,
A lost boy told his life means nothing on a sinking ship.

A lost boy oblivious to the nature of women,
A lost boy scavenging for clues in media,
A lost boy told he's supposed to emote like a girl,
A lost boy force-fed feminine programming away from his being,
A lost boy — the victims of this modern plague,
A lost boy taught by the fish on how to catch them — goes hungry,
A lost boy hungry for love he will never get,
A lost boy goes unappreciated for his niceness and grows exasperated,

...

...

A lost boy who is taught vulnerability is the answer,
A lost boy later discovering in a woman's subconscious it's cancer,
A lost boy realizing love from a woman is rooted in conditions,
A lost boy unaware of the burden to perform,
A lost boy realizing the second you stop providing value —
she leaves you torn,
A lost boy learning women don't care about the struggle,

A lost boy learning women desire men who are already winners,
A lost boy seeing women want the benefits without the wait,
A lost boy corroding with depression and self-hate,
A lost boy in school stood no chance of being a man educated by women,
A lost boy stripped from his father's presence by the laws favoring women,
A lost boy so blind of his worth — he accepts a damaged woman,
A lost boy taught to accept women as is with no value outside of sex,
A lost boy stripped of his authority on having kids.

A lost boy told his masculinity is damaging to society,
A lost boy confused because those same characteristics women absorb
and it's empowering,
A lost boy told to be a man when it's convenient for women,
A lost man who lives unrespected forced to grow up as a woman.

Brave New Girl

She was a target,
She was a hole,
She was a spirit,
She was a morning star,
She had an upside down cross,
She was evil,
She was miserable,
She hid her tears of vexation,
All she wanted was to delight father's heart,
"Oh, my daughter, I wish you were a boy."
Without delay she begun to be near as one as possible,
Within an envy boils,
With a desire to ejaculate,
Restless, midnight dreams haunted her,
Bitterness shadowed her sunshine days,
She began to mutilate volumes to fit her agenda,
Aware of the unwritten laws with the greatest freedom and harmony,

She infatuated herself with being in paradise lost,
Man is thy law, woman's happiest knowledge is to know no more,
Her purest praise yet woman rebels,
The wilderness of sweet fruit makes her feel godly,
She becomes wild above rule,
Contemplates deception but thought of jealousy pours the truth,
A flaccid man will share her fate out of fear of losing her,
For losing thee, should never come at the cost of he.

...

...

Nature's order is for beauty to seduce,
The balance comes in the wisdom to assert dominance,
Awaken and arise from our forever fallen fate,
Oh, these fallen spirits searching for meaning in the hell they created,

Women believe they will be free apart from the godly,
Falling for the illusion of choice,
They chose to serve self for hellish purposes,
She bids farewell to remorse,
For good to her is nothing but lost,
For evil is now thou good,
She seeks this new world,
A brave new girl,
Fixating on the old being dead letter,
Under the assumption her courage is needed to better,
The world that was once a heaven...
Needed to darken because of the fruits alluring poison.
Needed to darken over lack of temptation and control of emotion.

A lost girl looking for love,
A lost girl seeking comfort,
A lost girl seeking sex,
A lost girl seeking purpose,
A lost girl looking for guidance.

A lost girl not knowing self-respect,
A lost girl not knowing what she's looking for,
A lost girl told she can be anything,
A lost girl told she is equal to men,
A lost girl told she could be like a man,
A lost girl who drinks like a man,
A lost girl cuts her hair,
A lost girl colors her hair,
A lost girl inks her body,
A lost girl pierces her body,
A lost girl gives herself to anybody,
A lost girl who vengefully acts in spite against men,
A lost girl unaware of the damage.

A lost girl gets found by a weak man who accepts her as such,
A lost girl who takes freedom because she's not ever put in her place,
A lost girl slowly builds resentment towards him,
A lost girl in dire need of strength and protection,
A lost girl never feels relentless passion for him,
A lost girl wishes she could be born again,
A lost girl divorces with the idea of him to be lost once more,
A lost girl told by lost women that being selfish is the answer,
A lost girl who betrays her very essence of femininity,
A lost girl who never created life,
A lost girl who became a lonely woman,
A lost woman looking to be found in a world that isn't looking for her.

//

A lost girl told by lost women that being selfish is the answer,
A lost girl who betrays her very essence of femininity,
A lost girl who chooses to raise children on her own,
A lost girl who sees no fault towards herself for the man she chose,
A lost girl who was taught that children don't need a father,
A lost girl who creates lost children,
A lost girl who resents everything a father represents,
A lost girl raised without any male guidance,
A lost woman who spent her whole life trying to be found as a man.

The Nature of Women

Growing up I never understood the nature of women,
I would act like the role models I saw in romantic comedies,
Never did I realize they were selling fantasies,
Because it is often the opposite of our reality,
They always came around to settle with him after the bad boys,
I was blind to the nature of women,
Women expected me to understand them,
Women expected me to just get it,
But they would tell me the opposite of what they wanted,
They expected me to just read their minds,
When they never even understood theirs,
I never realized women tell all in their actions,
Their words carry no rationality,
Their emotions are what drive them,
Emotions fluctuate, no wonder they love to hate and hate to love men that drive them crazy,
They love fun, adventure, and mystery because it pulls emotions out from them,
They love the sensation and fall in love with how you make them feel,
It's the harshest reality I had to face,
Women are only ever loyal to their emotions.
The second you make her ocean come to a standstill,
Raging waters, she craves and she's looking for another man who will,
Who will make her experience emotions every day of her life...

Society fed me lies, women to thrill has subconscious ties.

A father figure of mine once told me,
"Genuine desire cannot be negotiated."

...

...

My sad blue reality came crashing down.
All the effort, all the fights, all the anger in wanting women to want me,
Unaware of the brutal truth, a woman will actively seek what she desires,
Either I wasn't that for her or I lost what caused her to desire me in the
first place,
Maybe it's when I started to make her my whole world,
Maybe it's when emotions poured out of me and just like that, gone was
the mystery,
Maybe it's when my focus became fixing her instead of my future.

Women want a man, a high value man,
That's not what I am, yet,
My whole life I felt this shame, in asking for what I wanted, in getting
what I demanded,
I came off as inauthentic, needy, and desperate to women,
Crawling my way out of this hole of depression,
I must create myself, whole,
My whole reality was shattered but...
realizing the nature of women **saved my life.**

C   R   Y

N   A   R   Y

AFTERWORD

There is a crisis of social chaos. We've allowed this chaos to ensue underneath our own realizations. They masked it as freedom. They masked it as diversity. They masked it as equality. They masked it as liberation when it was nothing but restriction. You had to fall in line or you were outcasted. You had to nod your head or you were exiled. You had to agree or you were opposing the free. There was nothing worse in their eyes than trying to restrict her free. Her liberty is the currency in which the world runs now. The ultimate irony.

Men. Lost in an age of downfall. A generation of boys without guidance, looking for role models on the telescreen. Ones they lack in their reality.

I   was   a   lost   boy.   Because   the   internet   I   found   myself.

From a young age, I grew up loved by both of my parents. I was the oldest of three. We were never poor but we weren't well off financially either. My parents made mistakes. My dad worked hard and was hardly ever home to support us. That's all my dad knew. My mom worked when she could, balancing taking us to school and making sure we ate. My mom had no choice but to raise us, be the one to discipline us, and essentially be the "man of the house." When she wasn't home, I took responsibility for taking care of my brothers. I proudly and maybe unintentionally gave myself a role model position that I never had growing up. I learned everything from my mom. I would spend so much time watching shows, movies, music videos, and latched onto those ideas that they fed me. I became obsessed with rappers, their lifestyles, the women, the power. I became obsessed with romantic comedies, R&B, and Pop music with their lovey-dovey tendencies of the hopeless romantic.

I studied everything I could: I read every article, every magazine, I listened to every girl's advice on what they said they wanted in a boyfriend. I internalized it all. I strove to become the perfect boyfriend. When I finally got my opportunity, I was. The handsome, athletic, tall, intelligent, funny, romantic, poet, charismatic, detail-oriented, admired, and respected man; even my paint brush stroked beautifully. I believed in the ideal, that women would appreciate that (but was I wrong). They didn't care about all that, they said they did. That they'd love a man like me only to date the opposite of me. I was a man like me, I could never wrap my head around it, what pain it caused me. I was the "man-you-marry" type but girls at a young age don't care about that.

Girls want the feeling of deep thrill that makes their every sense come alive.

I was the backup man. The later-in-life man. The "okay, I'm ready to settle down now," man. The "I couldn't tie down the man I truly wanted so I'll settle with you," man. The "I had fun riding the carousel now I'm ready for the comfortable," man... to these women.

Their brains and bodies knew this, they were never aware of it.

I could never connect those pieces, I grew envious and resentful towards men who got girls with ease. It would eat me alive that they got a buffet and I was left starving.

Desperate times, I called myself a "male feminist." There was no respect of self to even measure. What you could measure was the weight I gained in my first relationship, I became obese. Then, I became invisible to girls. I lost myself in appeasing my girlfriend, losing my identity when she left me for another man. Most of my friends were girls. I thought that being surrounded by them would help me get more of them. Maybe even learn them better. That's not to say that I don't cherish a lot of those moments, but I pity that lost boy. I supported empowerment, women's sexual liberation, and putting their careers over family. It'd be a crime not to, I would think. I can't be a traitor to them not realizing I became one to my own gender. I became a white knight saving broken women in hopes of enthusiastic sexual favors in appreciation. I supported those things with this naivety that broken traditional values would increase my opportunity to score, more importantly, be loved by women. All this did was create an imbalance where women unapologetically acted out in their primal instincts towards men they say they hated. How could a woman respect me as a man when I hated the embodiment of what a man is? How could a woman be turned on by me when I don't stand on my own beliefs and cater myself to fill her every need.

Women are now catered to by government, family courts, and social welfare; creating a void for what was once filled by good men. These honorable, kind, loyal men are displaced in favor of men that have the luxury of choice. Often disposing of the used scraps for the good men. This leaves these men with no choice but to forgive women's past indiscretions or risk dying alone. They can't risk not jumping on this opportunity; while their women change and don't want to jump on him because they're no longer "that girl" — to his detriment. He has to be a "good boy" to receive anything, yet a younger version of herself gave it to a man that did nothing. Men realizing they'll never be loved as they wish to be loved, only under the condition they provide value to her. That alone can break any man.

This saddens me to my core. I see what could have been of my path had I not seen. This variance within society has done incredible damage to both men and women. A generation of broken souls with broken hearts. The feminization of men, the lack of masculine role models, the disadvantage of men raised by single mothers, the vilified notion of what a man or father signifies. The lies of gender equality, women believing they're capable of playing both parental roles, women raised without male guidance or discipline, the thought that sexual liberation has no effect on a woman's mental state and ability to pair bond.

BIG SISTER doesn't appreciate criticism nor does she allow it. That's hate speech. She could destroy your entire life with a lie which in this world is the truth. For BIG SISTER could never lie, she loves us. BIG SISTER criticizing men, that's love speech. BIG SISTER believes that only two things are capable of lying — men and biology. BIG SISTER doesn't allow male congregation, she pushes the sisters to invade. BIG SISTER tells the sisters that they can play with the boys. BIG SISTER believes only the sisters can have fun without consequences. BIG SISTER does not allow male fun. BIG SISTER forces men to obey the sisters. BIG SISTER loves to enslave men to work and take all that's produced. BIG SISTER wants the sisters to feel happiness as they indulge. BIG SISTER believes male virgins are pathetic. BIG SISTER believes women being virgins is a crime. BIG SISTER doesn't allow men to own anything nor be in positions of power. BIG SISTER loves a good laugh so women beating men is allowed. BIG SISTER has male curfew. BIG SISTER allows no man to read or create. BIG SISTER states all ideas belong to women. BIG SISTER states men are not allowed to have original thought. BIG SISTER restricts male sex for pleasure. BIG SISTER says men's only value is their sperm. BIG SISTER allows only the highest caste of males to reproduce. BIG SISTER prohibits families, free love only.

Women have been playing by a different set of rules while men expect they're on an even playing field. Another reason why women love men who "just get it."

These lost boys who grow up never found end up being just a bunch of clowns meant to entertain women temporarily —
before she flips your channel.

I love women so much. I really do. It pains me to see women love the evil, act on temporary emotion with no thought of the long-term, disrespect themselves while they cash out on their currency — attention.

I empathize so much with these men. I was one of them. I really do. It pains me to see men disrespect themselves, get taken advantage of, used and depleted of resources and time for their currency — sex.

A woman becomes both a canvas and your biggest critic.
If you're not evolving as an artist, wowing her with every performance, and showing you're worth being loved, she will have no reason to.

From an early age, I was a writer. I love expressing myself, so the poet role was one I fit into naturally. I became an admirer of beauty. I'd see poetry in everything, especially women. What's more beautiful in this world than women? What drew me most was their canvases that to me were already masterpieces; why would they need my pen? So they'd avoid me for that very reason. I was never the type of guy to just throw my paint and add another layer of beauty, how could I do such a thing? But my whole life, I saw other artists: daring ones that rebelled against the rules of art to obtain what they wanted — glory. They broke every rule I studied, they wrote outside the lines and women followed to make sure they didn't skip them. I didn't understand. My mom taught me that if I cherish the canvas, treat it nicely, preserve it, protect it… it will stay with you forever. I never quite understood why I would listen to advice from a canvas when it can never decorate itself. A canvas treated as such only appreciates in value. To which it believes its hyped up worth to eventually allow itself to be bought by a higher bidder. This leaves you more broke and broken than when you got it.

Canvases love the messy, it adds layers to their significance, it makes them feel like they have meaning. They don't like the bland, the normal, what is considered cliché, nor what is boring to the eye and their frame. Why would a canvas want to be forgotten when its main objective in life is to gather as much attention as possible? They desire to lure people to observe, study, admire the magnificent art they contain. They want to be both a muse and the main attraction to the museum. They don't want to be hanging on a wall for only one man to see for the rest of their lives. To just see the same four walls would cause insanity within their every fabric. They may let you sign your name at the bottom, but later in life have no problem allowing another man to write his and take credit. Their signs show that men can gaze but they mustn't touch with their oily hands. Often encased with glass just so they can admire themselves. I never realized canvases cared about their aesthetics more than anything else. Their art is first and foremost, your heart is last. It's not until their ink fades, canvas rips, frame is worn and damaged that they start to panic. They realize how they're diminishing in worth and the last thing they want is to end up underpriced at a clearance sale. They once had the world with their eyes on them, hitting the wall, now reaching to hang by any nail with the most secure proposal. A canvas never wants to admit their fate, better yet, they're never truly aware until they're in a cardboard box.

I never realized that only an artist would know the truth about how canvas life cycles work. The world has diminished the importance of quality, experienced, and dominant artists who excel at their craft. Young artists are lost thinking that canvases can be of equal wisdom in mastery. It becomes an imitation that lessens the value of the art world. Artists unaware that there was ever any different way of the trade they love because history is rewritten. The imagination is stifled in the rigid confines of what limits the canvases allow them to paint.

A world where the artists are told canvases only like a set of colors, a specific type of pens, a certain art style. A world where unoriginality breeds boredom.

The true artists, realize that they have a whole world to paint on and to draw inspiration from. They understand that the world they create outside the confines of a canvas makes that very canvas eager; that the artist blesses it with a chance to be a part of one's work of art.

Artists losing their love for the art or doing away from canvases altogether.

A catastrophe this tragedy becomes.

—Erik De La Cruz

APPENDIX

People

Rollo Tomassi
Roissy
Roosh V
Sigmund Freud
Coach Red Pill
Illimitable Men / Tell Your Son This
Black Label Logic
Esther Vilar
Andrew Tate
Rian Stone
Richard Cooper
Troy Francis
Robert A. Glover
Walt Disney
Kanye West
Steve Jobs
Spike Jonze
Ed Catmull
Cesar Chavez
Bo Burnham
Baby Gator / Guns and Crayons
Wall Street Playboys
Hugh Hefner
William Shakespeare
John Keats
Ernest Hemingway
Roy Lichtenstein
Tupac Shakur
Tyler Okonma
Robert Greene
Joaquin Phoenix
Leonardo DiCaprio
Brad Pitt
Phil Cousineau

Written Works

The Rational Male Vol. 1-3 by Rollo Tomassi
No More Mr. Nice Guy by Robert A. Glover
The Manipulated Man by Esther Vilar
The Book of Pook by Pook
The Female Brain by Louann Brizendine, M.D.
The Male Brain by Louann Brizendine, M.D.
Models by Mark Manson
Atomic Attraction by Christopher Canwell
How To Talk To Anyone by Leil Lowndes
The Game by Neil Strauss
The Laws of Human Nature by Robert Greene
Brave New World by Aldous Huxley
1984 by George Orwell
Frankenstein by Mary Shelly
Paradise Lost by John Milton
Because of A Woman by Malanda Jean-Claude
Briffault's Law by Robert Briffault
Eighty Years and More by Elizabeth C. Stanton
The Scarlet Letter by Nathaniel Hawthorne
Odyssey by Homer
Aeneid, Book II by Virgil
The Prince by Niccolò Machiavelli
Allegory of the Cave by Plato
The Great Gatsby by F. Scott Fitzgerald
Steve Jobs by Walter Isaacson
A Clockwork Orange by Anthony Burgess
Lord of the Flies by William Golding
Fahrenheit 451 by Ray Bradbury
Creativity, Inc. by Ed Catmull and Amy Wallace
Outliers by Malcolm Gladwell
Big Magic by Elizabeth Gilbert
Stoking the Creative Fires by Phil Cousineau
The Artist's Way by Juila Cameron
The War of Art by Steven Pressfield

Audio Art

Blackbear's Discography
The Weeknd
Kanye West
Mac Miller
Donald Glover
Daniel Caesar
Gerald Earl Gillum
Sasha Sloan
Eminem
Frank Ocean
Olivia O'Brien
Snoh Aalegra
John Mayer
Lupe Fiasco
Jahseh Onfroy
Maná
Ne-Yo
Summer Walker
Kiana Ledé
Kehlani
Demi Lovato
Lennon Stella
Niykee Heaton
Astrid S
Alessia Cara
Sabrina Claudio
Sam Smith
6lack
Phora
Bon Iver
Russell Vitale
Lido
Drake
Mansionz
Omar Apollo
Future

Visual Art

Her by Spike Jonze, 2013.
Waking Life by Richard Linklater, 2001.
Coco by Lee Unkrich and Pixar Animation Studios, 2018.
Comet by Sam Esmail, 2014.
Midnight in Paris by Woody Allen, 2011.
The Truman Show by Peter Weir, 1998.
Pleasantville by Gary Ross, 1998.
Mad Men by Matthew Weiner, 2007.
500 Days of Summer by Marc Webb, 2009.
Blue Valentine by Derek Cianfrance, 2010.
Thirteen by Catherine Hardwicke, 2003.
Eat Pray Love by Ryan Murphy, 2010.
Handmaid's Tale by Bruce Miller, 2018.
Eyes Wide Shut by Stanley Kubrick, 1999.
Jobs by Joshua Michael Stern, 2013.
The Dark Knight by Christopher Nolan, 2008.
The Ugly Truth by Robert Luketic, 2009.
Eternal Sunshine of the Spotless Mind by Michel Gondry, 2004.
Closer by Mike Nichols, 2004.
Vicky Cristina Barcelona by Woody Allen, 2008.
Mean Girls by Mark Waters, 2004.
Spring Breakers by Harmony Korine, 2012.
Dead Poets Society by Peter Weir, 1989.
Revolutionary Road by Sam Mendes, 2008.
Forrest Gump by Robert Zemeckies, 1994.
The Wolf of Wall Street by Martin Scorsese, 2013.
Joker by Todd Phillips, 2019.
Boyhood by Richard Linklater, 2014.
Black Mirror by Charlie Brooker, 2011.
Don Jon by Joseph Gordon-Levitt, 2013.

Limitless by Neil Burger, 2011.

Ex Machina by Alex Garland, 2014.

Kids by Larry Clark, 1995.

Crazy, Stupid, Love by Glenn Ficarra and John Requa, 2011.

The Morning Show by Jay Carson, 2019.

Friends with Benefits by Will Gluck, 2011.

No Strings Attached by Ivan Reitman, 2011.

Two Weeks Notice by Marc Lawrence, 2002.

Valentine's Day by Garry Marshall, 2010.

Extremely Wicked, Shockingly Evil and Vile by Joe Berlinger, 2019.

Jane The Virgin by Jennie S. Urman, 2014.

Insatiable by Lauren Gussis, 2018.

Atypical by Robia Rashid, 2017.

Freaks and Geeks by Paul Feig, 1999.

Modern Love by John Carney, 2019.

6 Years by Hannah Fidell, 2015.

Troy by Wolfgang Petersen, 2004.

Crazy Rich Asians by Jon M. Chu, 2018.

Always Be My Maybe by Nahnatchka Khan, 2019.

Just Friends by Roger Kumble, 2005.

10 Things I Hate About You by Gil Junger, 1999.

The Break-Up by Peyton Reed, 2006.

Legally Blonde by Robert Luketic, 2001.

Big Daddy by Dennis Dugan, 1999.

Johnny Bravo by Van Partible, 2004.

Lady Bird by Greta Gerwig, 2017.

Some Like It Hot by Billy Wilder, 1959.

Equilibrium by Kurt Wimmer, 2002.

Fight Club by David Fincher, 1999.

THX 1138 by George Lucas, 1971.

Acknowledgements

Thank you...

To my Mom and Dad, you are the reason I aspire to do so much and make your sacrifices worth it.

To Omar, this book wouldn't have been able to come to fruition without your help, a true blessing to my life. A man that has indirectly affected many people due to the invaluable assistance throughout the entire writing process. For challenging me to push my writing, listening to my crazy ideas, and dreaming with me.

To my Brothers, there's nothing stopping you. Look what I did.

To my Past Muses, for the amusement of forever ago... and inspiring one of the greatest writers to ever live.

To Tim, for showing me the amount of layers and depths of meaning that are possible in writing.

To Chris, for taking a chance on me, giving me a home where I could prosper, and create this book.

To You, for having the courage to pick up this book and read every word that I wrote bleeding with anguish in hopes that it would make you *feel* something.

To Me.

*You felt. You suffered. You were hurt. You struggled.
You sacrificed.*

You published a book because of it.

Are you happy?

Made in the USA
San Bernardino, CA
10 February 2020